War Memorials of St Peter's Church, Old Woking

A Guide

Dr Anthony Morton

'We Will Remember Them...'

The vast majority of British War Memorials were dedicated after the end of the First World War, or Great War, as it was originally called, to commemorate the one million war dead of the British Empire. The unprecedented numbers of casualties suffered by Britain's armed forces and those of her empire during the war had a massive impact on villages, towns and cities throughout the country, with the result that after the war many thousands of memorials were set up to commemorate both the part played in the war by local communities and the local people who had been killed.

Another result of the trauma experienced by the nation, due to the huge losses sustained during the war, was the institution of Armistice Day ceremonies every year on the anniversary of the signing of the Armistice on 11 November 1918. At 11am on 11 November every year, almost all activity, whether private or public, was interrupted for two minutes to observe the Great Silence in memory of the dead. Formal ceremonies with prayers, the laying of wreaths at memorials and speeches were held in town squares, on village greens, in shops, offices, factories, schools and other places. Commemorating the war dead was in fact regarded as a sacred act and the 11 November became known as 'Armisticetide', giving it the air of an ancient religious tradition. For many the commemoration of the war dead was an intense emotional experience. In the first Armistice Day silence, it was reported that 'women sobbed and even men were moved to tears'.

After the Second World War with almost half a million British combatants and some 70,000 civilians dead,

fewer new memorials were built as in many cases the memorials to the Great War were adapted to recognise the later dead, often by adding the names of those who had died but sometimes simply by adding the inscription '1939–1945' to the memorial. In 1939 the two minutes silence had been moved to the nearest Sunday to 11 November so as not to interfere with wartime production.

After the end of the Second World War most Armistice Day events were moved to the same Sunday and both World Wars were commemorated. The day became known as Remembrance Day or Remembrance Sunday.

The year 2014 marks the one hundredth anniversary of the outbreak of the Great War and commemorations will be taking place in many different forms throughout Great Britain. This booklet seeks to remember and honour the war dead of Woking Parish who gave their lives for their country and community in both world wars.

The War Memorial Cross (Churchyard)

The design of war memorials set up after the First World War naturally reflected the character of the communities for whom they were made. It is not surprising, therefore, that in contrast to the Woking town war memorial, St Peter's Church chose to have a memorial in the shape of an antique Christian Cross.

In fact the 16ft-high cross, which was made of Cornish granite and stands in the churchyard opposite the church porch, is of Ionic design, so called because the design was traditionally associated with St Columba, an early Christian missionary who founded the abbey on Iona in 563 AD. The cross and its inscription were made by Messrs G Maile & Son of 367 Euston Road, London.

The inscription reads:

"To the Glory of God and in proud and loving memory of the men from this parish who gave their lives for their country in the Great War 1914–1919".

After the end of the Second World War the inscription *"1939–1945"* was added.

The WWI Memorial Tablet (Church Porch)

As early as February 1917, St Peter's Church Council had decided to create a permanent memorial to the war dead of the parish at an appropriate time in the future and to this end the Roll of Honour was maintained.

After the war a marble tablet recording the names of 78 men from the parish who died in the war was installed in the church porch at the same time as the war memorial cross and was also erected by Messrs G Maile & Son of 367 Euston Road, London.

The war memorial cross and tablet were unveiled and dedicated on Saturday 27 November 1920. The very well-attended service was held in the churchyard and conducted by the Vicar of St Peter's the Reverend George Askwith. Brigadier-General Charles Philip Scudamore CB CMG DSO on behalf of the Army and Admiral Thomas Philip Walker DSO on behalf of the Navy performed the unveiling ceremony together. Brigadier-General Scudamore had retired in 1910 after a long and distinguished military career that included

service in many colonial campaigns culminating in the Boer War of 1899–1902. During WWI he came out of retirement and by 1917 had become Deputy Adjutant General of the Egyptian Expeditionary Force. He had lived at Yarrowfield in Mayford, Woking since his (first) retirement. His son John, aged 19, died in France in 1915, while serving with the King's Royal Rifle Corps.

The Rural Dean, the Reverend Norman Paros MA, gave the address which ended with these stirring words: '*We long for a better England, and that England can only come, believe me, when its people give themselves in the spirit of Jesus Christ to this work. Carry away then, these three thoughts - remembrance of those who died, thanksgiving to God for his mercy, and finally dedication.*'

The WWII Memorial Tablet (Church Porch)

Known at the time as the Old Woking and Mayford War Memorial, the WWII Memorial Tablet was sponsored by the British Legion Westfield Branch who, with the full support of the vicar of St Peter's Church, the Reverend Reginald Heath, had suggested the idea in November 1947. At the time the secretary had expressed the hope that a book giving more details of the servicemen whose names were to be engraved on the memorial would be forthcoming (this would not be realised until 2007). The Woking Urban District War Memorial Committee helped to supply the casualty list. The Guildford Diocese issued a faculty authorising the installation of the memorial on 30 June 1949.

The funds were raised via public subscription. One of the local businesses that donated to the fund was Unwin Brothers (Gresham Press) whose directors gave £5-5s. Until 2007 Unwin Brothers was located in the High Street, Old Woking and is famous for having published JRR Tolkien's fantasy novels *The Hobbit* and *The Lord of the Rings*. The initial cost was £167-1s-10d for the tablet and engraving and 16s for the addition to the WWI Cross, followed by the later addition of a name to the WWII tablet that cost an extra 11s-8d. Enough funds were raised to leave £10 left over. This money was given to the church to be used for its clock.

The London Necropolis Company supplied and engraved the tablet of white marble with a *verde antico* border and fixed it below the WWI tablet in the church porch, after having moved the latter nine inches lower down to make room (otherwise the WWII tablet would be too high up the wall to read comfortably). The Company also engraved '1939–45' on the granite WWI War Memorial Cross in the churchyard.

After the 10.30 service on Remembrance Sunday 12 November 1950, the WWII memorial tablet was unveiled by Admiral of the Fleet the Lord Tovey GCB KBE DSO, who lived at Tormhun, Maybury Hill, Woking. The church was packed and garden chairs and benches had to be set up in the aisles. Having been given permission to do so by the Bishop of Guildford, the Admiral also gave the address, in which he lamented that the past 50 years of progress in social conditions, science and medicine had been thrown away in two world wars. He urged everyone to accept his responsibility not only as a citizen but as a Christian. He challenged his listeners by saying '*We have got to live Christianity every day of our lives, and we have to introduce it into our homes, our business and in our politics.*'

Admiral John Cronyn Tovey had had a vary active naval career in both world wars but was most famous for leading the Royal Navy task force that sunk the German battleship *Bismarck* in 1940. As Commander-in-Chief of the Home Fleet, Admiral Tovey would have been expected to direct operations from the Admiralty in London rather than risk his own safety but he chose to personally command the task force and led the hunt for the Bismarck from his flagship the battleship *HMS King George V*.

Personal WWI Tablets (North Wall of the Nave)

Five of the men who appear on the WWI Memorial Tablet are also commemorated on personal memorial plaques installed inside St Peter's Church on the north wall of the nave.

Major Laurence Elliot Booth MC and BAR was the fifth son of Frank Henry Arthur and Florence Booth of Hoe Place, Old Woking. Aged 26, he was killed at his guns while in command of a Royal Field Artillery Battery near the small Belgian village of Neuve Eglise on 13 April 1918 during the Battle of the Lys. Previously he had been wounded (in April 1917) and twice mentioned in despatches. He is buried in the Heuvelland with Vlaanderen Cemetery, 13km south of Ypres (Grave 1VA9). The plaque was erected by the officers and men of his Battery.

The Latin inscription 'DULCE ET DECORUM EST PRO PATRIA MORI' at the foot of the tablet is taken from a poem by the Roman poet Horace (Ode III.2.13) and translates as '*How sweet and right it is to die for one's country*'.

Lt Edward Selby Wise was the son of Edward and Amy Wise of 2 St John's Road, Bexhill-on-Sea, previously living at 'Whitegates', Loop Road, Kingfield, Woking. Aged 27, he was killed in action on 20 October 1914 near Nieuport in Belgium, while leading his men who had been landed from his ship the monitor *HMS Severn* to assist Belgian forces. He is buried in the Ramscapelle Road Military Cemetery, 2km east of Nieuport (Grave 1VA3). The plaque also commemorates his brother **Lt Stacey Wise**, aged 22, who died on 22 September 1914 when his ship the cruiser *HMS Cressy* was sunk along with two other cruisers of the Seventh Cruiser Squadron, *HMS Hogue* and *HMS Aboukir*, by the German submarine U-9 in the region of the southern North Sea known as the 'Broad Fourteens' off the Dutch Coast. Lt Stacey Wise is listed on the Chatham Navy War Memorial set up for those Royal Navy personnel with no known grave (Grave Ref 1).

The poetry inscribed in the bottom right hand corner of the tablet reads as follows:
So from the hearth the children flee,
By that almighty hand
Austerely led; so one by sea
Goes forth, and one by land:
Nor aught of all man's sons
escapes from that command.

The text is the fifth verse from the poem '*It is not yours, O Mother,….*' by Robert Louis Stevenson. The Latin phrase 'PRO PATRIA' beneath the figure of St George translates as '*For one's country*'.

Captain Francis Hardinge Follett Booth was the third son of Frank Henry Arthur and Florence Booth of Hoe Place, Old Woking. Aged 28, he was hit while leading A Company of the Second Battalion of the Worcestershire Regiment against a German counterattack near Gheluvelt in Flanders on 25 September 1917. His body was never found and he is listed on Panel 75/77 of the Tyne Cot Memorial to the Missing in Belgium. The plaque was installed by his family and includes his brother Laurence Elliot Booth.

The Latin inscription 'GLORIA IN EXCELSIS' at the top of the plaque is a shortened form of "*Gloria in Excelsis Deo*", which translates as 'Glory to God on high'.

The Latin inscription 'QUOD ERO SPERO' at the foot of the tablet means '*I shall be what I hope to be*' and is the family motto of the ancient Booth family.

Private Percy Francis Taylor 235962 was the son of Arthur and Margaret Taylor of Westfield Cottage, Westfield, Woking. Aged 37, he died of wounds on 1 May 1918 while a prisoner of war at Tournai in Belgium. He may have been wounded and taken prisoner during the Battle of the Lys in April 1918 when his unit, the 9th (Northumberland Hussars Yeomanry) Battalion

(previously known as 9th Battalion Northumberland Fusiliers) suffered heavy casualties. He is buried in Tournai Communal Cemetery, Allied Extension, Tournai, Hainault, Belgium (Grave 11 B4).

The phrase '…Life….more abundantly' at the foot of the tablet is a severely truncated form of the second half of the biblical verse "*I am come that they might have life, and that they might have it more abundantly*" taken from John's Gospel 10:10 (King James Version).

The WWI White Ensign

A brass plaque beneath the small medieval window in the north-east corner of the nave commemorates the presentation in early 1919 of a White Ensign rescued from a Royal Navy warship that had fought during the war and been commanded by Admiral Thomas Philip Walker DSO, a Churchwarden (People's Warden) of St Peter's for 25 years from 1908 to 1932.

Having retired as a Rear-Admiral in 1908, he had his patrol vessel, the armed yacht *HMS Aegusa* (Pendant No 082), sunk under him during the war while he served in the Auxiliary Patrol Service, having been given a temporary Commission as a Captain in the Royal Naval Reserve. The *Aegusa* hit a mine laid by the German submarine U-73 off Malta on 28 April 1916 with the loss of six lives while looking for survivors of *HMS Nasturtium* that had also been lost to mines from the same U-boat. In 1917, Walker was advanced to the rank of Admiral on the Retired List. In recognition of his services "in the prosecution of the war", Walker was appointed a Companion of the Distinguished Service Order on 3 June, 1918. The White Ensign from *HMS Aegusa* was originally laid up in this corner but was later moved to the back of the gallery to avoid being damaged by the newly installed lighting system. Admiral Walker also presented a Union Jack to the Church. It is highly probable that both the White Ensign and the Union Jack were the ones used to cover the Memorial Cross before it was unveiled.

A second brass plaque behind the pulpit on the east wall of the nave was installed by Admiral Walker's family and friends on the occasion of his death on 27 August 1932. They also paid to have the church bells tuned in his honour. Admiral Walker, who had lived at Homeleigh in Mount Hermon Road, Woking since 1896, was such a prominent citizen of Woking that his funeral at St Peter's Church was a huge affair with many military and civilian dignitaries in attendance. The Admiral had been a keen bell ringer at St Peter's and his colleagues rang the bells fully muffled before the service in his honour. Admiral Walker was buried in Old Woking Cemetery (Grave 967 Plot 3) on 30 August 1932.

Above:
Admiral Walker and the brass plaque installed at St Peter's on his passing.

Above (from left):
Stand of flags (south-east corner of nave); stand of flags (north-east corner of south aisle); the three flags of the Zouche Gallery.

Stand of flags (north-east corner of the south aisle)

The two flags displayed in this corner of the south aisle are, from left to right, the Standard of the British Legion Women's Section Westfield and District Branch, and the Standard of the 1940 Dunkirk Veterans Association Woking Branch. The latter was laid up in the south aisle in June 1993. The 1940 Dunkirk Veterans Association was one of the first ex-Service organisations to be formed from personnel who served in the British Armed Forces during the Second World War. It was founded in 1953 'to assist all needy members and their families and to foster the spirit of comradeship that existed on and off the Dunkirk beaches in 1940'. It was disbanded on 30 June 2000 because of the declining numbers of surviving Dunkirk veterans.

Stand of flags (south-east corner of the south aisle)

These three flags, from left to right, include a very old British Legion Westfield and District Branch Standard, a Royal Naval Association Woking Branch Standard, and a newer Standard of the British Legion Westfield and District Branch laid up on 29 June 2004. The British Legion was founded in 1921 to represent ex-servicemen and women. It became the Royal British Legion upon receiving a Royal Charter on 29 May 1971. It provides support for ex-service personnel and their families and in various ways works to keep alive the traditions of the original Armistice Day in national life. The Royal Naval Association received its Royal Charter in 1954 and provides support for ex-service personnel and their families from all branches of the Naval Service. The Woking Branch of the Royal Naval Association parade at St Peter's Church at the annual St George's Day Service, held on the Sunday closest to 23 April, St George's Day.

Stand of flags (Zouche Gallery)

These three flags representing the three armed services were originally laid up around the chancel arch but were moved upstairs to the rear of the gallery on 25 January 2005 to avoid being damaged by a newly installed lighting system. The White Ensign and Union Jack were presented by Admiral Walker (see above) and the RAF flag, dedicated on Remembrance Sunday 1952, was presented to the church by Air Commodore Claude McClean Vincent CB CBE DFC AFC. Air Commodore (later Air Vice-Marshal) Vincent had been Air Officer in Charge of Administration, Fighter Command from 1949 to 1952. During the First World War he had served in the Army and the Royal Flying Corps, and in the Second World War he served with the Royal Air Force in the Middle East. He died at Farnham in Surrey on 8 August 1967 aged 71.

(Photo: Crown Copyright.)

Left:
Air Commodore Claude McClean Vincent CB CBE DFC AFC, who presented the RAF flag now situated in the Zouche Gallery.

Right:
Captain Walker's ship, shown here as SY Erin before being converted to military use (including being equipped with two 3-inch guns) and renamed HMS Aegusa.

Bottom:
Admiral of the Fleet the Lord Tovey GCB KBE DSO, who lived in Maybury Hill, Woking, unveiled the WWII memorial tablet at St Peter's Church on Remembrance Sunday 12 November 1950.

Old Woking Burial Ground

Most of the individuals named on the WWI and WWII memorial tablets in the church porch died while serving overseas and are buried in the relevant military cemeteries in the region where they died. A few, however, died while in the United Kingdom and are buried in the Old Woking Burial Ground close to St Peter's Churchyard. Sadly, in some cases the circumstances of their deaths are unknown.

Gunner Godfrey Beale boarded with Thomas Stocker, a carpenter, and his wife Mary, at 'Cricketers' Cottages, Westfield, Woking, before the First World War. Aged 26, he died on 9 November 1918 while serving with the Royal Field Artillery, two days before the Armistice was signed.

Sapper Alfred W Bird 556453 was the husband of Clara Bird of 114 High Street, Old Woking. Aged 35, he died on 1 February 1919 while serving with the Royal Engineers.

Private Stephen Burchett 1118238 was the son of Albert and Annie Burchett of 49 Westfield Square, Woking. Aged 23, he died in England on 27 May 1944 while serving with the Pioneer Corps. He is buried in Plot 4 Grave 1487.

Private Eric W Green 5504206 was the son of William Charles and Esther Mary Green of 147 Church Street, Woking. Aged 25, he died in England on 22 December 1942 while serving with the 2nd/4th Battalion Hampshire Regiment. He is buried in Plot 3 Grave 1422.

Gunner Albert Morris Inwood 2354 was the son of Rosa Inwood and the late David Inwood of Walnut Tree Cottage, Moor Lane, Westfield, Woking. Aged 26, he died of wounds at home on 29 June 1915 while serving with the Royal Garrison Artillery. He is buried near the east boundary of the burial ground.

Private Thomas Inwood L/8170 was the son of Rosa Inwood, and the husband of Mrs L Inwood of Market Cottages, Old Woking. Aged 28, he died of wounds possibly sustained during the Battle of Loos (28 September–16 October 1915) on 24 October 1915 while serving with the 1st Battalion The Queen's Royal (West Surrey) Regiment. He is mentioned on his brother Albert's gravestone but is in fact buried in Grave 111 A4 Longuenesse (St Omer) Souvencir Cemetery, Commune of St Omer, Pas de Calais, France.

Private Philip Reginald James Long 6090080 was the son of William Richard and Emily Long of 11 Quatermaine Avenue, Westfield, Woking. Aged 21, he died on 8 September 1941 on anti-invasion duties in East Anglia while serving with the Queen's Royal Regiment (West Surrey). He is buried in Plot 3 Grave 1263.

Sergeant John Patrick Martin 13071197 was the son of Thomas and Sarah Martin of 35 Gloster Road, Old Woking. Aged 38, he died on 1 December 1945 while serving in the Pioneer Corps. He is buried in Plot 4 Grave 1578.

Private Christopher May G/35462 was the husband of Helen Edith May of 10 Beaconsfield Road, Kingfield, Woking. Aged 41, he died on 18 June 1920 while serving with the 11th Battalion Sussex Regiment (Labour Corps) transferred to 650462 Prisoner of War Company. He is buried in the north-west part of the burial ground.

War graves from Old Woking Burial Ground (clockwise from top left):

Sapper Alfred W Bird 556453
Private Eric W Green 5504206
Private James Thorpe G/3671
Sergeant John Patrick Martin 13071197
Gunner Albert Morris Inwood 2354
and Private Thomas Inwood L/8170
Private Christopher May G/35462
Aircraftman 1st Class Neville Wade 1236350

Graves from Old Woking Burial Ground (right):

Lt Stacey Wise RN
Lt Edward Selby Wise RN
Admiral Thomas Philip Walker DSO

Aircraftman 1st Class Ronald Shoesmith 1606926 was the son of Harry and Florence Shoesmith of Omega, Moor Lane, Woking. Aged 20, he died on 8 May 1944 while serving with the Royal Air Force Volunteer Reserve as an Air Charge Hand/Under Training/Air Gunner with 7 Air Gunners School under Flying Training Command. He was on board Anson aircraft serial number LV300 that was lost after a mid-air collision with another Anson serial number MG131 near Glamorgan. He is buried with his sister Thelma in Plot 4 Joint Grave 1488.

Aircraftwoman 2nd Class Thelma Joan Shoesmith 2160052 was the daughter Harry and Florence Shoesmith of Omega, Moor Lane, Woking. Aged 18, she died of natural causes on 5 June 1944 while serving with the Women's Auxiliary Air Force as an Air Charge Hand/Wireless Operator with 13 Radio School under Technical Training Command. She is buried with her brother Ronald in Plot 4 Joint Grave 1488.

Gunner Arthur Ernest Simmonds 942386 was the son of Joseph Edward and Evelyn Minnie Simmonds of 54 High Street, Old Woking. Aged 24, he died on 29 October 1943 while serving in the Royal Artillery. He is buried in Plot 4 Grave 1455.

Private James Thorpe G/3671 was the husband of Jessie Thorpe of 17 Westfield Square, Woking. Aged 51, he died on 24 June 1915 while serving with the 2nd/5th Battalion Queen's Royal (West Surrey) Regiment, possibly during training in England. He is buried in Grave 486 in the South-West corner of the burial ground with his son Alfred James, who died aged 25 on 2 October 1916.

Aircraftman 1st Class Neville Wade 1236350 was the son of Timothy and Winifred Rose Wade of 42 Council Cottages, Westfield Road, Westfield, Woking. Aged 21, he died on 10 November 1943 while serving in the Royal Air Force Volunteer Reserve as a Wireless Operator with 1660 CU (Conversion Unit) under Bomber Command. He was on board a Lancaster Heavy Bomber Serial No ED812 that crashed at RAF Dunholme Lodge in Lincolnshire after losing its tail. He is buried in Plot 4 Grave 1458.

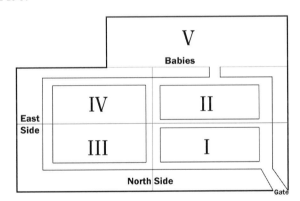

Directions to Old Woking Burial Ground

Leave your car in the Church car park in Church Street. Walking, turn right out of Church Street and walk along to Life Works (the large house on the bend). Take the track down the right side of this house until you reach the Burial Ground on the right.

The Burial Ground is basically divided into five main plots plus the north side (adjacent to the fence going left from gate); east side (far left-down the fence); west side (down the fence to the right of the gate). The paths form the boundaries to the plots. Standing at the gate, ignore the path to the left and walk straight along the path in front of you until you come to the next dividing path on the left. Turn and face down this path. The area bounded by paths on your left is Plot 1; Plot 2 is on your right. Continue down this path between Plots 1 and 2 until you reach the next through path; across this path the area to your left is Plot 3 and to your right Plot 4. Retrace your steps to the first path running from the gate and turn left. Plot 5 is beyond Plots 2 and 4.

Index of Names – World War I

ALLARD, STANLEY
ATKIN-BERRY, HAROLD HARDING
BEALE, GODFREY
BIGWOOD, JOHN
BIRD, ALFRED W
BOOTHE, FRANCIS HARDINGE FOLLETT
BOOTH, LAURENCE ELLIOT
BULLEN, ROBERT
BULLOCK, ALFRED
CANHAM, ARTHUR
CANNONS, FRANK
CHORLEY, PERCY
CLARK (E), JOHN
COLE, CHARLES ARCHIBALD
COLLIER, ALBERT
CRANE, JOSEPH
DABORN, HORACE JOHN
DABORN, JOHN
DENCH, ERNEST EDWARD
EDES, WILLIAM
FOSTER, BERNARD La TROBE
FOWLER, THOMAS AMOS
FREEMANTLE, JAMES ANNELS
FULLER, WILLIAM BLYTH
GALE, THOMAS HENRY
GILES, WILLIAM
GORTON, THOMAS
GUNNER, SAMSON ALBERT
GUNNER, WILLIAM
HAMPTON, DICK TERREY
HARDING, GEORGE HENRY
HAYES, WILLIAM
HEATH, EDWIN
HEATH, F
HOAD, ALBERT
HOAD, FRED
HOWARD, WILLIAM
INWOOD, ALBERT, MORRIS
INWOOD, THOMAS
JELLY, ALBERT, GEORGE
KENT, CECIL (or CYRIL) GEOFFREY

KENT, CLIFFORD
LORING, GEORGE, FREDERICK
MARCH, HENRY STANLEY
MAY, CHRISTOPHER
MUNDAY, SILAS
PASCOE, JOHN MYDHOPE
PHILIPS, WILLIAM
PINK, FREDERICK HENRY
PIXLEY, REGINALD GEORGE HOWELL
REED, ALFRED JOHN
REED, GEORGE ALFRED
RITCHIE, FRANCIS JAMES DICKSON
ROLFE, RAYMOND HAROLD
ROLFE. WILFRED OWEN
SALE, ALBERT
SALE, WALTER JOHN
SAVIDGE, JACK DOUGLAS
SCUDAMORE, JOHN
SHOESMITH, FRED
SMITH, ALFRED
STENT, WILLIAM EDWARD
STEVENS, CHARLES WILLIAM
STEVENS, DENNIS
STEVENS, JOSEPH
STEVENS, WILLIAM
STEWART, THOMAS COOPER
STREET, ERNEST
SULIVAN, HENRY ERNEST
SULIVAN, PHILLIP HAMILTON
TAYLOR, PERCY FRANCIS
THORPE, ALFRED JAMES
THORPE, JAMES
TUCKER, FREDERICK St GEORGE
WAITE, ARTHUR E J
WEBBER, ERNEST
WILLIAMS, ALBERT
WILLIS, GEORGE F
WISE, EDWARD, SELBY
WISE, STACEY
WORSFOLD, WILLIAM HENRY

BAKER, STANLEY
BARNETT, ERNEST FREDERICK
BRADSHAW, SIDNEY EDWARD
BRAGG, JOHN HALL
BROWNE, HENRY CHARLES
BURCHETT, STEPHEN
CEELEY, ARTHUR FREDERICK
COLLYER, HAROLD
COOPER, DENYS A
DABORN, LEONARD BASIL
DAVIES, CHARLES FREDERICK
DIMMICK, DAVID ROWLANDS
EDMED, KENNETH ROY
FOX, SIDNEY HORACE
FULLER, CHARLES WILLIAM
GEARY, LEONARD WILLIAM CHARLES
GREEN, ERIC WILLIAM
GRIFFIN, COLIN
HART, MARGARET VICTORIA
HAYTER, EDWARD WILLIAM
HOLLINS, A J F
JELLEY, STANLEY ARTHUR
JONES, ROBERT CHARLES Wm
De KOCK, JOHANNES WILLIAM
LEE, GEORGE WILLIAM
LEWIS, LIONEL MORLEY
LONG, PHILLIP REGINALD JAMES
LONGHURST, LESLIE
MACDONALD, HAMISH WHEELER
MARKHAM, ARTHUR J
MARTIN, ARNOLD WALTER
MARTIN, JOHN PATRICK

MAY, GEOFFREY TRELAWNEY
POWELL, ROLAND ANSELL
RIDER, REGINALD
ROGERS, VICTOR ALBERT
ROLLINSON, GEORGE LESLIE
RUSSELL, LESLIE RONALD
SHEARS, GEORGE ALFRED
SHELLEY, JOHN THOMAS
SHOEBRIDGE, GEORGE CECIL ERNEST
SHOESMITH, RONALD
SHOESMITH, THELMA
SHORTER, EDWIN CHARLES
SIMMONDS, ARTHUR ERNEST
STEVENS, THOMAS OLIVER
STRUDWICK, PERCIVAL
TAPLIN, JOHN HENRY
TARRANT, EDWARD CECIL
THATCHER, DOUGLAS EDWARD ALLAN
TOVEY, FREDERICK WILLIAM
TOWNSEND, TERENCE HENRY
TOY, ARTHUR JOHN
TRUSCOTT, JACK ALBERT
TYRRELL, GEORGE FREDERICK
UNDERHILL, JOHN WILLIAM
WADE, NEVILLE
WARNER, HAROLD
WELLS, GEORGE
WICKENS, STANLEY EDWARD AUSTIN
WILLIS, GEORGE GEOFFREY LIGHTLY
WOOD, RONALD CHARLES
WOODHOUSE, JOHN BERNARD
WOODS, COLIN JAMES BERNARD

*Private Horace Brotherwood, aged 18, of 1 Elm View, Goldsworth Road, Woking is missing from the WWI memorial tablet. He served in the Army Service Corps (711 MT Company) and took part in the first ever tank attack in history. He was part of the crew of tank C1 'Champagne' (No 721 Male) during the attack on the village of Courcelette in support of Canadian forces on 15 September 1916. His tank ditched while following a German communications trench and he was killed by enemy shrapnel as the crew abandoned the tank. Private Brotherwood is buried at Pozieres British Cemetery in France. Two other crew members, Sergeant Fred Saker and Gunner George Lloyd, both serving in the Motor Machine Gun Service, were also from Woking and survived the war.

Bibliography

Air of Authority - A History of RAF Organisation, *http://www.rafweb.org/Biographies/VincentC.htm*

Banks, Arthur, *A Military Atlas of the First World War*, Leo Cooper 1989 (reprint)

Boorman, Derek, *A Century of Remembrance*, Pen and Sword 2005

Clyde Built database, *http://www.clydesite.co.uk/clydebuilt/viewship.asp?id=18998*

Commonwealth War Graves Commission, *http://www.cwgc.org/find-war-dead.aspx?cpage=1&sort=name&order=asc*

Hawkins, Nancy & Smith, Margaret, *The men of World Wars 1 and 2: remembered with honour on the war memorial of St Peter's Church, Old Woking*, self-published 2007*

Haythornthwaite, Philip J, *The World War One Source Book*, Arms and Armour Press 1997 (reprint)

King, Alex, *Memorials of the Great War in Britain*, Berg 1998

National Archives, *1911 Census*

National Archives, *Walker, Thomas Philip, Rear-Admiral*, ADM 196/39/605

National Archives, *Walker, Thomas Philip, Admiral*, ADM 196/87/54

St Peter's Church log book

Surrey History Centre, minutes of St Peter's annual Parochial Church and Vestry meetings, ref 5172/2/1

Surrey History Centre, papers relating to Old Woking WWII War Memorial, ref 1228

The First Tank Crews, *www.firsttankcrews.com.*

The Times, *Air Vice-Marshal C McL Vincent* (obituary), 11 August 1967

The War Graves Photographic Project, *Scudamore, John, http://twgpp.org/information.php?id=3345489*

The Worcestershire Regiment, *www.worcestershireregiment.com/bat_2_1917.php*

Surrey History Centre, Woking Electoral Registers 1915, 1920, 1953

Woking News and Mail, *Cross and Tablet unveiled-An Impressive Ceremony*, 3 December 1920

Woking News and Mail, *Death of Admiral T P Walker-A Distinguished Naval Career*, 2 September 1932

Woking News and Mail, *Vast Gathering at Old Woking-Memorial Unveiled by Lord Tovey*, 17 November 1950

Woking Parish Church Monthly Magazine, November 1950

Wreck Site, *http://www.wrecksite.eu/wreck.aspx?37135*

Young, Vivian, *The Village and the Church of Old Woking*, 1948 (offprint from St Peter's Church parish magazine)

* A copy of this publication is kept at St Peter's Church and another is held at the Surrey History Centre.
If you would like more detailed information about St Peter's and its local history, extensive records are held at the Surrey History Centre in Woking.

Dr Anthony Morton, March 2014